Moondogs
&friends

poems by
~~Andrew G. Carrigan~~
[signature: Andrew L. Carrigan]

*For Charmaine,
as in Maine, cool rocks
bubbling like the
as enduring an
inspiration as always
Andrew
River Kathy
9/29/12*

Saline, Michigan • 2012

©2012 Andrew G. Carrigan All rights reserved.

No part of the contents of this publication may be reproduced, stored in a retrieval system, or transmitted in any form or by any means, electronic, mechanical, photocopying, recording or otherwise, without the prior permission of the author.

ISBN 978-1-300-03418-6

PRINTED IN USA

*for jude, arlene, and maggie,
without whom this collection would not exist.*

Also by the poet:

Too Sweet to be True • Press Lorentz online, 2009

Sex Instructor Retired • Limited Mailing Press, 1993

The King • Crowfoot Press, 1981

To Read To Read • Crowfoot Press, 1981

You Poems • Crowfoot Press, 1979

The Threshold of Heaven • Crowfoot Press, 1978

Babyburgers • Street Fiction Press, 1975

Book 3 • Sumac Press, 1972

MOONSHINE

we hate the sun rising in the east
it is too bright to gaze upon
with our loving eyes   so we rise up
and walk toward the western horizon
where soon enough the sun slides down
and venus fixes us with a steady stare
she is suspicious   but detecting
the purity of our hearts
she passes us on to jupiter
and finally the brightest natural light
of the night sky   we are walking by now
in our bare little dew washed feet
the earth slows at a perfect spot
we stop   curl up   and gaze and
gaze and gaze
moondogs of reflected light

CONTENTS

- DRUMMER ... 7
- FIRMAMENT ... 10
- ODE TO ODES ... 11
- ODE TO SANITATION ... 13
- WEATHER CONTINUES EVEN IN SPRING ... 14
- THE AMHERST LADY ... 15
- ANOTHER ONE FOR YOU ... 16
- HUMMINGBIRD EGGS ... 17
- MEXICO CITY ... 18
- HALFBACK ... 19
- SONGS OF THE HEART ... 20
- PERFECT MISTAKES ... 21
- SPECULATIONS BY MYSELF ... 22
- BIG HITTER ... 23
- HAS BEEN ... 24
- YOU CERTIANLY KNOW THE RIGHT THING TO WEAR ... 25
- PAEAN ... 26
- TODAY'S LESSON ... 27
- MY HEART ... 28
- I SUSPECT ... 29
- OPTIONS IN THREE PARTS: PSALM, HANGOVER, AH HA! ... 30
- CURTISS PARK, MAY 8, 2011 ... 31
- BLESS YOU MY CHILD ... 32
- FALSE DAWN II ... 33
- READING ROOM ... 34
- ROYAL WEDDING POMP AND TREAT ... 35
- FULL-LENGTH WHITE SHELL ... 37
- STAN! ... 38
- THE GHOST OF MARILYN MONROE ... 40
- ANGELS WEEP ... 42
- WEIMMARRHINER ... 43
- BROKEN HEARTS ... 44
- DOUBLE-DOG DANG ... 45

DONALD TRUMP HAS A BRIDGE FOR SALE: AN EPIC	46
I DON'T HAVE TO	47
RESIGNATION	48
ACROPHOBIA	49
BLESSÉD ART THY DÉJÀ VOUS	50
JUNE 5, 2011, EARLY MORNING	51
ERUDICITY	52
ANXIETY	53
BLACK HOLES	54
TIME TO KILL	56
TODAY, TOO	57
ANOTHER MORNING	59
(POEM)	61
WONDERS ARE THERE MANY	62
A LOVE TRAVELOGUE	64
HE UNDRESSES A PART OF HIMSELF HE THINKS	65
AND, WELL, SO, WHAT ABOUT LOVE?	66
ANOTHER YOU POEM	68
SAY	69
WORDS	71
WINTER DREAMS	72
SOGGY FOG MORNING	73
RICHARD POEM	74
LESSONS LEARNED AGAIN	75
INVITE	76
HERON IN THE HURON	77
COFFEE-STAIN BROWN	78
TUESDAY I THINK IT WAS	79
THE DAY BEFORE MY SEVENTY-SEVENTH BIRTHDAY	80
UPON THE POND	82
APRIL IN ~~PARIS~~ SALINE	83
Acknowledgements	85
About the Author	87

DRUMMER

1.
i know you! you have brains
we haven't even used yet
your head full of *moon moon*

leave us reconnoiter

if all insects were to suddenly disappear
within fifty years all life on earth would vanish

if all human-beings were to suddenly disappear
within fifty years all life would flourish
                              jonas salk
surely we can do better than that   leave us
ruminate together
mind you insects have some strong advantages
they multiply like rabbits   most are small enough to
avoid detection   many work day and night
without rest   they have no parties or distractions
and only the queens have reproductive responsibilities
we on the other hand have nothing but distractions
iphones texting sweets drinks constant assault by
sexual innuendoes and commercials   keeping
in touch in general plotting advantages and takeovers
moving ahead with a united beneficial plan seems to
skip our genome entirely leaving us our *angst*
our *humanum est errare* things do not look too spiffy
yet from our current despair with political and economic
leaders responding entirely to cold hard cash
we do suffer deeply from their aloofness
the *blah blah blah blah* in the news media
why don't they just shut up and tell the truth?
why don't they understand we just want to adore them?
trust them?

we don't learn from history! never have!
that's why we leave it to their *superio*r intellect
       we know we are under attack
       we know the peacemakers lack patriotism
       we know they expose the country to danger
we have it down to a knee-jerk
we ignore the plank in the eye for the forest
but where are the trees?
there is an escalator around here somewhere
but is it up or down?   surrounded by dark anxieties
the dark is silent   it can hardly hold the
tiny light of stars
the moon plunged over the horizon an hour ago
it (the dark) is full of animals talking to demons
they come closer wanting to use our voice too

2.
while the lord himself appeared to be focusing all his
attention on the miraculous performances in sports
and we thus distracted
he really took advantage with a sky-dome trick
see   we are the leftover genetics that spoiled creation
incomplete in his own image   ADHD without
forethought   definitely nemesis bound
he tried to dismiss us because we are fully half-baked
but he can't dismiss his own brain
even for mental errors
now we are here   trapped in global warming
we will add the carbon monoxide ourselves
and go on display while the lord himself
says to the others
"see their frozen gestures as if they were just
going to speak   aren't they precious?
maybe a wish or a paean of awe
i do miss them so   like friday fish"

yaagh! sorry   my brain is such a knot
i would stop now but it goes on
trying to find a friend   as in *cartagena*
our white-knuckled hands clamped together
eyes filled with each other
we leapt to our feet and kissed
across the table   it sparkled
and we knew outrageously
perfect joy for twenty minutes or
so   not bad
the afterglow of *cartagena* is here
with me now   sitting alone
in the *aura inn* at clear lake
alternating tequila and beer
it walks the afternoon sun
across the bleached hardwood floor
whoa! the cantina musicians
the same yip and pluck
near-joy nonsense to relax the pinch
in nostrils and sinuses   nothing more
nothing important   just something to do
while we're here

FIRMAMENT

if it hadn't been for her extravagantly beautiful legs
and windy hair   no one would have invited greta
the narrow mountain paths   obviously the music of
aida in the background   and finally the center court
machu picchu at dawn   if only dikembe mutombo
had not been traded to the white sox right before the
jai alai playoffs   we needed more than a fourth-round
draft pick   so we sat starving and alone
until greta began to paint an abstract chiaroscuro mural
using only the sun moving along the wall as a template
and too much of one pigment we thought
but the ancients loved it   coming out of the moss to
greet us   handing out multi-colored beanies with earflaps
perfect for the high night air
tropical fruit for breakfast   vegetables at noon
they were all mesmerized by the whir of her dove-like
fingers highlighting the symbols during the exegesis

then the priests showed up   offered a small infant sacrifice
before the evening's line dancing to a cool reed pipe
as a finale the elders invited greta to mount the heavens
and take her place among the stars   where her twinkling
would rule over them always

such gratitude from the losers   we were speechless
she thanked them with her ankles

ODE TO ODES

1.
"i've ode you this ever so long"
she says   "you've languished
in my debt so comfortably
you on the couch   me dangling
my fingers in the bidet
slowly of a sudden i knew
what it was i wanted
but how to bring it about?
for the longest time i hummed
quietly into a tissue paper and comb
adding a note each time until it
rang in my head like a tune
when it was ready i committed it
to an orange still life in pewter bowl
the most musical of all musical tins
how often i've longed to return
to those days with cello strings
the promising lilt both for and from you"

2.
"in my younger days"   i say
"i played and practiced by ear so long
with a few easy flaps i could rise
above the highest telephone poles
many of the shorter oak trees
and open bedroom windows
then my scalp gave way
and i lost the ability to grow hair
it was at that time i took to slouching
in the setting sun   sifting m&ms
through my fingers   palm to palm
until dusk finished what is left of day
and i turn on a low lamp

over a cup of coffee i realize
(the sky aflame with false dawn
and birdly twitters)
this is a delicately fragile and fragrant
cacophony of life inside and out
how the blood leaps in my heart and brains
while a chorus of sopranos holds off at
ppppp the universal love song of star nurseries
i accompany with rachmaninoff of the large hands
sad though it was   an ode to be heard only once
and you asleep"

ODE TO SANITATION

most bathrooms are so small
you can wash your hands while you sit
or gaze at the perfection that is your face
as it turns from attractive pose to pose
oh it delivers perfect mirror images
while i watch   but where does it go?
i mean when i exit stage right   how
do i know it doesn't exit stage left?
i quickly dart a look but too late
it has moved on
which introduces an old fear that has
just occurred to me   what if my real
face left my face as i slept   like an old
forgotten halloween mask at christmas?
and became a wandering vagabond
that stumbles into love with a sleek bay
filly   gleaming in the morning sun
somewhere in kentucky
and she quivers with anticipation
ears erect as i approach
huge chrysanthemums of steam
blossom from her nostrils
oh how love would mount to the sky
like icarus the greek
or that other wingéd horse on the mobile
sign   rising high and higher with gas prices
until the climatic "little death"
as the romantics called it   then back to earth
where i am so sad at the distance i must walk
to light her cigarette after and when i do get there
there is a nicotine patch on her chin!

WEATHER CONTINUES EVEN IN SPRING

i love what you've done with the snow
even more than being a slimy toad
the smooth undulations form various shades of lavender
to mauve backed by cerulean twinkle
yes much better i'm sure
though you were very descriptive in your rant
very like my junior year abroad at corsham england
a glorious old estate
that failed under the constraint of child-labor laws
still they had a *ha-ha* to keep the cattle on the grounds
and peacocks with brilliant metallic-blue fur and peahens even
every day we sang *god save the queen* under the rustle of spreading
leaves and the headmaster read a prayer from the official
book   what would *jesus* say?
i thought it blasphemous though no lightning struck
it was there i had my first taste of lead and mercury in art class
in rhetoric musty quills gave me blurry-eyed tears
and a throat closed to breathing   just as your cruelty clutched
my heart with its boney fingers   and it swooned
when i awoke the grip of your flabby fingers remained even to this beat
though i promise never to again   i'm sure you'll never forgive me
so   please   allow me to grovel even as i will

THE AMHERST LADY

"effervescent evanescence" emily said
"the hatpin of stars   that's the ticket"
the amherst lady one instructor called her

well   people were different back then
the times were different   slower
people had time to say *evanescent effervescence*
or whatever she said   it's true i'm sure
like the yiddish radio comedian used to say
"dit you effer see eet vhen eet effer vasn't?"
probably from vaudeville   most were
he said it every week   next ting you know
efferbody say it

but in contemporary times what with cell phones
high speed internet and all   no one has time for
real words   and elegant wit
just time for words with one syl--

ANOTHER ONE FOR YOU

made an omelet with a double-yoked wren's egg
this morning   used a flat toothpick for a spatula
the cheese and garlic pretty much covered it   but
the flavor hung in there   i liked that   sort of
reminiscent of a white morel but more exotic
full of tiny bubbles that would have been chatter-song
in the characteristic tail-tilted-up pose
never mind how i found the egg or knew it was
           double-yoked

this is not what i wanted   i was thinking more of
something like you in a thin print dress from late '30's
before the war   clinging nicely to your shapes
moving or staying
you long and loose in the chair   on the couch
maybe the nail of your index finger between your front
teeth momentarily
all your expressions perfect wan smiles
after a while you think "all this languid posing in fantasies
is a bit boring with wren's eggs around"   then   "no   it's
okay"
it is okay

HUMMINGBIRD EGGS

your quail eggs are many many times the size
of hummingbird eggs
the strange thing is it takes exactly the same
number of each to make a really good four-person
omelet   some mix the two when they run short
i think this a bad idea
though both are delicate and superb
the flavors do not complement one another
and i do so hate a war of eggs when sharing
a sunny sunday morning repast with neighbors
            don't you?
so for heaven's sake exert yourself
find enough of one or the other when entertaining
it is a challenge at times   but so worth the effort

i've never really found a totally satisfactory use
for quail eggshells   the best i can do is grind them up
and sprinkle them on the seed mix in the feeder
good calcium
save the halves of hummingbird eggshells though
keep them on crushed velvet   preferably black
and use them to serve *benedictine!*

MEXICO CITY

YUK! two tongues dancing in one mouth
soothing   stroking   slathering   all
dark   slime and saliva
the scene raises the question
why two tongues in one mouth?
one connected at the root and wagging its tail
tasting of lemon curd
the other   limply mauled   gives the reason
it is a slice of boiled beef tongue served for dinner
the livelier one presses against the roof
squeezes out the juice   sucks   and swallows
places the other neatly between the teeth
and the teeth grind sensuous as a steamship
lips pursed in an   *mmmmmmmmm*
the rooted one dreams of *veracruz* shining in the sun
of *acapulco* and the moon on the diving cliffs
red pumps with heel strap and stiletto heels clicking
in dance to a clicking conversation
with a naked pygmy from the bush
hand on top of his head as the heart pumps
its red message of heat to their glands
they click on   tickety-tick tickety-tic
not knowing they are in a garden in *las cruces*
clicking on not knowing which tongue is tasting which

HALFBACK

they use axle grease instead of bag balm in the udder barn
milk leaking from cracks in the roto-rooter
beyond the parlor many prairie lands   mountains beyond
a few hills between   candy and maryjane around the burbs
and the many inner city slums painted anew
here former fields of ethanol now sorghum stored in
left-over pales from the age of renovation
she was a farmer's daughter on the lam with a slicker
and barn boots headed east for the trip over the great waters
glitchy gloomy style after we hocked all our cash
on the steeper upper slopes she ran along side the dogs
stabbing ice from between their toes with pinking scissors
in the clear morning light a hedge of peonies
the unemployed sat on the top rail legs crossed at the knees
elbows rested there nicotine dripping from their soggy butts
relief came in the form of bathist mound builders
diamonds after
in the high church   oh 3 maybe 4 stories up   the priests
prepared oatmeal for the eucharist
accompanied by empty stomachs   they all agreed there was
no other way   sometime before this a head fake had put
the all-stater on his knees and it looked clear sailing
to the championship especially when norm came ambling over
from the right looking over my shoulder at someone
who might be approaching   it was the final touchdown
of the season   ice storms kept me from the banquet
we disguised the diamonds in sparkling bead curtains
the sun screaming in   35-40 degrees

SONGS OF THE HEART

all right you asshole break my heart like i
must have broken yours years ago to be treated thisa way
i often think but seldom eviscerate orally
unless alone in an enraged weekender
it made one person cry salty tears   all these years
but no one ever gave a shit about him anyway
my favorite device is to repeat words   lines
or phrases while i await the next descent from heaven
my favorite device is to repeat words   lines
or phrases while i *et cetera et cetera*

other times i just skip a line when crowds get
ugly with devices or poetics
this was at the time the last steamship on its final voyage
was someone sick over there awhile ago? maybe
my son uses yet another device: lean back in a deck chair
and squish waves on the horizon between thumb and
forefinger   sighting with one eye only   to ensure
happy trails!

PERFECT MISTAKES

spring came with the end of the year
just before the great explosion of smaller individual explosions
like the first night of year of the rat or pig or wolf
agnes was perplexed and wanted to say so
i had important business across town to get to late
the great chain of being sometimes clanks like marley's ghost
before it screams   there had been pedagogic masterpieces
surely   sparks propelling the apprentice beyond the masters
and horrific failures   dull dull miscues on all sides
maybe even a few perfect mistakes   agnes was the last shooed
out after a soft "may i talk to you?" business   important
business to be late to across town right now   not now
the great chain of being rattling on both sides of golden mean
top of the stairs   agnes on the landing halfway down next to the
railing where it turns for the return trip on down and out
looked back into my eyes   clung for a second *you let me down*
among all the other bobbing   swirling
then disappeared into the others   the look still hanging in the air
abandoned   hanging on and on   she was right you know   no doubt
what is it exactly we see when we think we see but don't
the polar bear is not white   the bluebird blue
even though we know   we think we see   fill in miscues
next morning driving into the parking lot   someone
has left a coat or field hockey bag   some lump
on the playing field   mistakes had surrounded her   her's and others'
perfectly seamless mistakes

SPECULATIONS BY MYSELF

every minute i spend with you i envy myself
that's the way it works on this planet
the outside of it anyway   very personal and private
not at all like planets we fly to in dreams
where we see poorly because we are asleep but know
threats on all sides the full knowledge deprived of us
like the mind of god and his guessing game
and it turns out mythological surface romances
on venus   real hot stuff   i like that
orange in color   supple and titillating
in a strange way   like sex in amphorae
to keep the salt out   reducing positions to three
but we can do better than that in a solitary journey
through space   circling and awestruck by
ringed planets   star nurseries   event horizons
munching on small handfuls of quarks
consider for example fractals or phi spirals
the golden ratio   golden mean   and the favorite
of politicians   the golden angle   a bar on the corner
in the city that houses
secret sessions with on-liners pockets bulging with
cash in phi-nomenonal square root exam scores

BIG HITTER

before kong was king kong he was just kong
to the locals   with whom he shared "candy" and
big combats deep in the dank swamps that lasted days
then the natives got a toehold along the beach
and formed a gated community the hellenes
might have admired had it not been a lost island
the locals in their turn formed a country club
and excluded the natives and everyone was satisfied
until a few white guys showed up in a boat
kong got the king kong moniker when he proved to be
the clear champion and all-time great at
hit the ball and drag fay hit the ball and drag fay

HAS BEEN

nothing sadder than a has been who never has been
beloved of children and pleasantly shaped lanky women
ambling confidently down the street in that
he'll be there when i get back the bastard way
jugs duking it out with a tight tiger t-shirt with "revolution"
printed on the front in script
he joined an egyptian dig to meet women with brains
and tireless work ethic to match his own
and it worked well enough in khaki shorts and shirt
tied in a knot in front to show his midriff and small
tattoo of a barn swallow about eight inches right of his naval
which always got the babes
that coughed hysterically in the desert dust for practice
but the lanky girls often recalled him to their mind
and had their button been able to turn them even a
quarter turn around they might see over the heads
of children playing kick-the-can with a coke bottle
there in the south u. street   someone they could
kick the can with and mooch drinks and drugs from
until true true love whistled them all home again

YOU CERTAINLY KNOW THE RIGHT THING TO WEAR

there was the moon bright white against the boathouse   a softer tone
on the lake totally becalmed   only the sound of small waves lapping the
sand twenty or thirty feet away   hardly a sound at all really in its own way
there were bright stars in the sky   the roofs of cottages like daylight
on the opposite side of the lake   and we thought individual trees beside
them it was so bright

the moon went down spectacularly at the southwest corner of the lake
even the shy stars came out then   the only sound the *wooooooo*
of raccoons we thought was their way of singing "moonlight
becomes you" but were later that afternoon to decide
was a kind of growling that only sounds like song   what a way
to live   darker now we thought it a perfect setting for touch
for a long time

until the sky grew light long before false dawn   and we could feel trembling
in our hearts   the gentle song of the mute swans all the way to our toes
and a small giggle or two at the tingling of our skin
how could we not   but awkwardly   kiss

PAEAN

thoughts of you have brought me thus far
bumping into streets   doors   the odd inner wall
a song of glitz and sunshine showering everything
with light and good health and moral vigor
before writing this morning i made a list words
stolen from other writers to use
   paean   fauna   limousine   agh   las cruces   bums (blush)
hallucinations are boring this morning
if you'd like to take part   underline the words
you think i listed with your favorite quill   those who blot them
with magic marker will be immediately enraptured!
then my pen put itself to paper and typed
after that we spent the afternoon sipping wine and
watching the descending sun arrange dust motes
on the carpet   magazines   coffee table
and edge of shadows
i wanted to use *you* in every line as i have used you
(so beastly) in dreams both asleep and insomniac
when we could see only passing auto lights on the ceiling
so at last you have me where you want me
out of your life   much like a boring figure of speech
or worse yet   one no longer in use   a waste   (waist!)
i would like to have you in more of my lines in many ways
"just hold your horses!"   john wayne?   no   my mother
whenever i needed slowing down or brought up short
like now   another favorite   *lord a massy!*
(*god! i-wanna-see-ya!*)
oneirocriticism?
onomatopoeia?

TODAY'S LESSON

he presents his lines in genteel generosity
erudite and slim as if badly loved
most of the words we recognize
though from other locals
often the case with others too
every so often without thinking we think
oh! that poem ends a line earlier
then we catch ourself embarrassed   humiliated
biting the tongue of consciousness   face
glowing beet red in the lamplight

MY HEART

my heart's tougher than your heart
and my heart is going to crush yours
with its finery gifts
except i haven't the stomach for it
or guts if you prefer
you see the opening like a blade
without a feint you slip me a winky-twinky
down low   i feel the jolt in every joint
my eyes tunnel through the floor into
an embracing black abyss   weightless
my last words
i should have stuck with my heart
i know i could have won

I SUSPECT

i know what you mean
i know what you intend
i know what you want!
my hope in this matter is a flock
of flamingos leaving key west for paris
and a weekend of shrimp almondine
à la mode   rich in omega threes
though around here we love our smaller
birds for humility   the bluebird   the baltimore
oriole   seldom seen   preferring seclusion in
leafy branches of deciduous trees   as if in
apology for the imagined gaudiness of their
neon plumage   or out of fear we might
crush them to our hearts in gleeful joy if
such pleasures exist!
                              like them   i fear you
for the beats you have stolen from my heart
the gushes of its titillated valves
was it just yesterday or an eon ago
you touch my hand to point out children
at play   and the thrill strips all plaque
and sends blood rushing anew
why shouldn't we celebrate our testimonies
with loop-dee-loops along the *aurora borealis*
quick hips flashing the luminosity of our painted nails
click-click   click-click   against the sun
then roar as we fall backward   terminal velocity
hell bent earthward
through our own incredible   undeniable beauty

**OPTIONS IN THREE PARTS:
    PSALM, HANGOVER, AH HA!**

1.
i was birthed alone
grew up alone surrounded by others
even now when i go out
i prefer the low-light of pool tables
the splash of brightly colored balls on green
the occasional beer bottle over the head
only when i chalk my cue
smooth the sweat with talc
can i really see who we are
three hundred million
eight balls in a corner pocket

2.
A MANIFESTO: FRIVOLITY
discover the world in frivolity
live in frivolity
exit in frivolity

3.
EPITAPH
struck down by octogenarian
driving while texting her grandmother

PS HIGH UP CURTISS PARK
saw a baltimore oriole
in full plume morning sun
(no glove no batting helmet)

CURTISS PARK, MAY 8, 2011

a bluebird watches from a red-bark willow
along the river bank   decides we are close
enough   takes refuge with altitude
in a black walnut   fifteen feet up
a crow with a crust touches down on the bridge
railing   sees us and continues on through the
limbs of silver maples along the opposite bank
stirring territorial flight among those too small
to identify   the commotion continues down river
tree to tree   around the bend and over the ridge
into the baseball parking lot
finally a pair of herons stagger their liftoff from
breakfast waters   fly low over distant trees
birds settle back in the branches   quiet
then warble territorial anthems   enjoy
a few more seconds of sunrise

BLESS YOU MY CHILD

suddenly i feel like a beatified pope!
it was earlier this morning in the light before dawn
yes i think this is what it would feel like   sort of a
serene holier-than-thou smugness   contentment
beyond any cardinal's comprehension
upper bureaucratic know nothings   huh
i walk out on the front deck beaming and i'm quite
sure glowing just a little   kiss the birds at the feeder
ha! this one *is* a cardinal   and here is his concubine!
how perfect   i practice about three minutes of the
arms out   palms up   *all you peasants off*
the grass routine i have always loved
much more expressive than the royal wave in england
then turn   return to the seclusion of the living room
the walls crawling with putti breath   then on
to the kitchen where i boil up some german noodles
for tonight's tuna-oodle casserole   fix a pot of zen
green tea and toy with the thought of texting jesus
for tea and biscuits   but decide against it   solitude
is the thing   solitude and thoughts of you   so pleased
for me   and why not?   the morning bursting with
blessings and tuna-oodle for dinner   i even consider
bringing back the friday fish fry!

FALSE DAWN II

the sky ablaze with orange and reds
false dawn this morning
accompanied by host on host of
angelic choirs practicing for the rapture

magnificent!   magnificat!   very nice

as the sky tucks away its enormous colors
for a bland blue-gray
there was a voice!

very nice   very nice this morning
it's coming along   be sure to vocalize
thoroughly before tomorrow's rehearsal!

apparently we have another day

READING ROOM

just finished reading again a favorite collection of poems
by a well-known author   i say poems and not poetry
because only those who dislike poems say poetry
students and golfers say "i never liked poetry"
aren't such sheltered lives sad in the extreme   i weep for them
too i now only re-read my favorite writers   contemporaries
seem not up to snuff   even those who are among my favorites
still alive seem to have taken a step back toward oblivion
the tried and true are best for me   ever faithful

i wash my hands thoroughly   and brush my teeth
lately i've been using three electronic toothbrushes
the first is a sort of sonic vibrator   the second a wildly
spinning polisher   and the third promises a thirty second smile
each has its charm   all do their duty   i use all three
at least once a day   twice on a good day
try on several smiles   none lasts a fun thirty seconds
i use all three because it has been nearly a year since personal
reasons have kept me from the dentists office and i hate plaque
i hate even more the hygienist digging and scraping at my gums
oh she is young and shapely and i don't mind her sitting on my lap
nor her flush boobs crushing my chest victor mature style
i mean marlene dietrich style   legs entwined for grip
i hate that   though right now i can't think why
halitosis?   moist lips? bedroom eyes? insomnia?

way back on mayday   that's three days ago
a day that will live in infinity   held in the pit of my darkest
personal humiliations and personal rendition self-abuses

ROYAL WEDDING POMP AND TREAT

1.
our saint sir disney could not have been more proud
without the polish of our cult of personality to flatten
what we could see on screen without comment
barbara walters   diane sawyer   et al of media blitz
were spell-binding   ugly american style

true   prince william's wave was full of tension and
            nervous twitch
lacking the reserve and dignity of a *real* royal wave
but he has years to work on that
it did not lack genuine courtesy and enthusiasm
fitting for the moment and those returning good wishes
even if the proceedings had lacked u.s. input
it did not lack glamour   genuine affection and what we lack
in royal eloquence
the clergy did get lost in round after round of
well written and pith-worthy prayers a bit
but the pageantry surrounding the happy couple
made us feel happily-ever-after begins now
if ever at all

2.
what if *our* princess di had been a foot to
eighteen inches shorter in height?
what would the world have been?
first of all she would have been a ballerina
filled with music   dance   joy
she would never have met the royals
and burned magnificently in their fire
but spun her magnificence in movements
across the stage and life
freeing us of the tragedy we know so well
but what would we have lost?
this wonderful day of promise rising from her ashes

benediction:
oh lord
you have made us of shortcomings
and given us imperfect tools
to work happy miracles
let us turn away from your royal we
let the knots of failure filling this life
unravel in full without memory
of you   or we   or anything

FULL-LENGTH WHITE SHELL

i'm first to admit it was kate's sister
who stole my heart and other sex
organs at the wedding
who would believe a full-length sheath
could contain such smooth organic curves
could she parade for me just so forever   no
far better to be the sheath itself
holding and caressing her every move   to breathe
with her breath as she goes about her tasks
could i ever allow her to leave
the full-length mirror while i watch
too soon weak from the sublime   we swoon together
till the rapture call

STAN!

put those poems down!
get to work on your writing
the stuff that brings in money!
well   except for what you do *pro*
bono publico   a term invented by
the idle rich in ancient rome
while making love to neighbors'
slaves   a silly way to make money
seems to me   what about the family?
don't they deserve to eat too?
not everyone can be erudite and slim
with a handsomely trimmed cookie duster!
you used to love my poems
because they loved you
but now you devour them smugnatiously
as you glide along on their surface sludge
in your kayak you've aptly named
superior to carrigan and see if i care
our friendship and love was so strong
it will outlast both of us and our progeny
we'll have to see about the cookie duster

but seriously about the money   cash   wampum
how are you to pay for my breakfast
delivered by the delicate hands of the tattooed
waitress your patronage employs for the good
of her *whistler's mother* type mother waiting
waiting in the gray and black chair arrangement
for the doggy bags each night?
don't you think her thighs ache with anticipation?
her heels tapping out secret messages to german
u-boats deep at sea because no one told her
they had all been sunk with the frantic screams
of captain and crew ending the war?

think about it as you slavishly give in to your least whim
reading poems for chuckles instead of calligraphically
in your beautiful hand   scratching out name cards for
the old farts you had so much fun with in high school?

(you may notice i have added something here
my latest invention i call *punctuation* because those
are the letters i had left   the squiggly one over a fly speck
i call a *question mark*   i've decided to use it only after
questions   isn't that neat?)

THE GHOST OF MARILYN MONROE

it was just a few minutes ago   maybe yesterday
last week?   thursday   it was thursday last
i was in second grade thinking how cruel life is
absolutely beyond despair for everyone who wasn't me
oh the girls liked me well enough   but the boys thought
i looked more and more like a punching bag
and by the time they were through with me i was
oh they held nothing against me but their fists
so it was not just simple cruelty
soon i was afraid of girls   afraid one might
touch my hand in finger-painting
or try to walk me home after school and the boys
might see us and make me hang by my fingers
from a nearby tree limb until my shoulders ached
while they practiced punching bag   oh it was no
good for her to cry and carry on on my behalf
it only infuriated the boys to punch harder
why was life so heartless for me and no one else?

one afternoon i saw marilyn monroe walking
down the street toward me   but no it was just my
recurring dream of niagara in her red satin dress
she always said *hello* in that phony stage
voice as if she were rehearsing
she was always warm and sympathetic at first
but as she slowly removed my clothes   she practiced
the wide-eyed-open-mouth shock thing
as she saw the bruises and lumps of healed rib fractures
her eyebrows quivered up and down up and down   she
repeated in her breathy best   *oh dear   oh dear
how did this happen   how did this happen*
in her carefully crafted stage whisper careful to
pronounce each sound of each word completely an amateur
she touched each wound gently with her fingertips

as if playing an accordion
her eyebrows quivered up and down and knitted
together in a wrinkle on the bridge of her nose
and every time i could see she was having ideas
ideas of her own as she gently wrapped my fingers
around a nearby tree limb   my toes barely touching grass

ANGELS WEEP

what kind of angst is this?
angels weeping for the deceased when we die
one would think angels had more insight to
life everlasting   i do anyway
why would they weep?
is heaven getting too full for them to spread
their wings as in the past?
the father's house has many mansions
and room for plenty more i'll bet
i can't buy the overcrowding thing

they say angels weeping at the "little death"
perfect sex   when the earth moves the angels are
overcome with ecstatic joy   they weep for that joy
sure   that's cool   unusual but could be true

but when the loss is ours and we weep for hours
at least we know we are weeping for ourselves
our loss   but the angels have lost nothing
or are they weeping for us and our loss
that's mighty suspicious   arrogant even
i've heard angels find our holier-than-thou
arrogance disgusting
and this weeping at dying thing is an example
of why they normally hold their noses around us
it is our stinking angst   not theirs
these egotistical   self-serving   fabrications of angels
is all very degrading and annoying
i won't buy it
shroud your bloody looking-glass for shame

WEIMMARRHINER

our neighbor has a rescue dog
a fully grown adult weimmarrhiner
or something like that
he confessed to us the other day his
real name is clarence and not casper
as his first cruel owner called him
imagine a handsome beast like himself
named after a cartoon character   ugh!
cruelty knows no bounds
he says being a rescue dog is okay
but there are cats in the house
they're okay   if they get smart-alecky
he stands on a tail with one paw
they can't do much then but do his
nails   they get along
babs   his new owner   our neighbor
is not as big as clarence   so he does
pretty much as he pleases on walks
babs is nice   small but gritty
so he never drags her far
"she's nice" he explains
when we meet on walks and i say
"hi clarence"
he immediately turns away
and goes to point on a distant woods
as if "clarence" weren't his real name
he tries to make us think he sees something
over there   a fawn or turkey
or maybe a rabid cat

BROKEN HEARTS

your vanilla coat flaps in a strong wind
as i watch you walk away down the sidewalk
but there is no wind   just you and your coat
and innocent pedestrians being bumped aside
you can't wait to get away   to get out of it
my life   that is   where you had been caged
in adoration

soon tears blur my peripheral vision
finally i see only what i assume is your motion
flouncing along   coat's color   like you   gone
what was it?   scarlet? royal blue? black?
no   never black   maybe grey with black
velvet collar   no   probably the canary yellow
trench coat i love   picked up at the dick tracy emporium
with tess trueheart

       suddenly my tears are so luxurious
my eyes flop from their sockets and plop
on the sidewalk   quickly scuttle to the side
 turn in unison   and   sadly   begin to stair up
women's skirts

prune face!

DOUBLE-DOG DANG

double-dog dang!
too late for us
the high priests of politics
have already sharpened the
obsidian blades of sacrifice
while we fiddled away
reality shows and fast food menus
all we can do is grunt up the deep
steps of the economy
grumbling about our misfortunes
the lesson we learn   if any   is
we have still lazy weaknesses
we do not or *will* not understand
the inexorable laws of nemesis
the goddess of retribution
arrogance and greed her main fair
coupled with our stupidity
we   the electorate   elected
nemesis taps her watch
there will be no *deus ex machina*
no god descending like a spider
from on high to save us
no *deus vult*   it is *we* who willed it
those are not angels circling   nor eagles
but the buzzards of our own filth
descending   double-dog dang!
to pick us clean

**DONALD TRUMP HAS A BRIDGE
FOR SALE: AN EPIC**

sing thalia and melpomene   daughters of zeus and mnemosyne
of the great wind that swept saline in the summer of '010
taking tree limbs   trees themselves   and electricity
the ground saturated for days
the cleanup weeks and months
how along the line of lilacs   between curtis park
and weller's carriage house   where amy and i walk each morning
a hole in the line of blossoms
seemed uprooted by the maelstrom
a jaw-dropping event in any weather   never heard of since
but not until after the leaves fell in fall was the ten-inch diameter
tree revealed which clearly had carried the lilacs with it
much later in winter a saw and its apprentice took the tree by truck
of no help to the lilacs   until just this morning amy and i noticed
someone had tried to replace the lilac roots in the ground
where they might thrive again   (good luck!)
just goes to show what   a standard fool i am   bite on the first
the simplest   the easiest answer without a further thought
as if everything in the universe were as simple as the tea party
as if half vast thoughts didn't lead to cranial malfunctions:
cling to the easy answer and hide hidden agendas
what a dunce   a dope   a darling dupe   invest in bridges
now that political maelstroms are
scrambling voters' alleged brains
demonstrate why democracy doesn't work

I DON'T HAVE TO

i don't have to do this
i could watch television for example
consider the possibilities of a new bra
discover a new cereal to shape a
new day between my teeth
or consider a pill that promises
a private bathtub for everyone
maybe watch a drama in which the secret
impulses of all characters
lead to complications   threats
and disasters on all sides
women beaten and raped and murdered
while loved ones are forced to watch
because society has created another slavering
monster who remains undetectable to authorities
the sort of thing we wade through
every day at large and undetected
in the primordial tide
we dogpaddle through in society
once in a while a handhold
where we rest and breathe in gulps
against huge swells
before we launch out wildly again
in that dark glandular flow--
the sea of *you* and *me*

RESIGNATION

okay   i won't make love or even try to   to you
until i know how   these things are not learned from victorians
might as well apologize to the rest while i'm at it
sorry
it is such a good idea too i think   love making not just feeling
then i joined the convent as a father confessor
all the women there so beautifully un-lip-sticked of the world
so like little buttercups   even the elderly
one died at 110 and i swear she was as flower-like as ever
did you ever hear about saint albans when in latter days
WOMPFFF! an underground passageway
between the convent and the monastery collapsed
we of the true church could always keep a secret if nothing else
there have always been a few real honeys too
their lovely hands and lips   oh this is heaven i think
just to be in their presence as their fingers caress the tapers
i encourage many to deliver their dreams in chapters
to fill in all details   so shy their innocence as they enjoyed
wonderful wonderful innocent and glorious revelations
of the lord our god and sinless savior

ACROPHOBIA

the superstructure of the universe is such dizzying heights
it should be measured in dizzying heights
our position in the milky way galaxy is seven billion
dizzying heights from the black hole at its center
the next closest galaxy is thirteen quadrillion dizzying
heights away   these comparisons of course make no more
sense to us than *love your fellow man* or *love thy neighbor
as thyself*   who in his/her right mind ever really loved itself
we are surrounded by walls of black holes on all sides
if you listen carefully you can hear them smacking their lips
as they gobble up light speed   static on your mobile

no wonder then that acrophobics shrink back to our tiny
planet and sink their noses in a good book
which means whatever you imagine as long as others
keep themselves out of your space   but they never do
people have their own inner dizzying heights
and that is why there are so many
religions   churches   temples   gods   saints   and etc.
and they are all true and accurate pre and post assumptions
worth dying or killing for   no wonder space physicists and
mathematicians   mystics and ethicists are led to new
arithmetics to fit us in

BLESSÉD ART THY DÉJÁ VOUS

we'd live in the high mountains
perfectly alone in wind and quiet air
where the morning sun on snow is like
late afternoon sun on the buildings of rome
we would live on *seul l'amour* of course
authentic left bank parisian-style
when we do from time to time leave the fire
to step outside and rekindle the starry sky
        then disappear around the corner of our chalet
        to meet once again at the door
as if many many years had passed
our passions aroused anew
and stoned on high thin air

JUNE 5, 2011, EARLY MORNING

the sun came screaming in so hot and heavy this morning
i had to squint my ears   i did appreciate it though
three days in a row of perfect sunrise
after so many days of rain all of saline was drawing up
plans and ordering lumber for arks   chelsea lumber
was swamped with 40 fathoms of backorders
the 24 hour lines were unrelenting   they were
finally able to close last night   just before the big dance
was it only 39 days of rain?

i of course   faithful as gravity   left wanting
wanting   wanting to touch it all
but could only gaze and gaze at the huge trees with a
gazillion leaves at the end of their branches
where the sun landed so softly they were unmoved
even the cardinals and orioles were silent

the sun screams in at a thirty degree angle at first
in the tops of trees   by thirty-five degrees
it blesses the graves on the hilltop of the old section
of oakwood cemetery   finally everything glows
the only green that can take morning by the scruff
shake it until everything is green awake   eyes blinking
i want to touch it all with my fingers   to feel the
sun arrive on leaves   but it can only be felt by full lungs
full full full   as the coffee cups at the drowsy parrot

ERUDICITY

gunna start including french quotes
popular in conversational english
in most or nearly all the works
this should give them the feel of erudition
slender and well schooled
it's really *slender* i'm after
and you can't beat erudition for weight loss
so again i'll have that look in every posture
of careless   casual repose   waiting at a corner
for example   everyone catches her breath
"who is *that!*" they all murmur
my nose at a perfect angle   not too high
that's haughty   just a charming angle
inviting surrender i used to get in any line
of course i'll have to keep them out of readings
there is no greater collapse than careless
accent in someone's favorite *hauteur*
there's a book with a list of them around here
somewhere   unless it's the one susan tore up
and threw in my face last night
"you're too haughty by half for my taste"
she said   the pieces around me like the
tickets of disappointed racing *aficionados*
i've always found susan's taste exquisite
so move my right hip back two inches
which lowered my nose near perfection
i close my eyes and see a murmur of women
gather round in a perfection of female grace
"how *erudite*" i hear them say
"how   *slender!*"

ANXIETY

arrogance and vanity are sure markers for ignorance
and all three are close on the tail of boredom
the greatest of the 8 deadly sins   i walk into a
coffee shop and everybody there i know   which is most
suddenly put their coats on   stop by and say   "have to take
mom to the mortuary by 3:00   she's thawing in the trunk"
"forgot my husbands water just broke   we'll talk"   or
"rest room here is jammed   gotta go down the corner"
suspicions easily allied with   "they know my new book
is out"   "my wit is too much for a belly laugh on a full tum"
humph   they're all gay or lesbians   lucky bastards
i've learned to enjoy a really good cup of solitary coffee
but contrary to a rumor going round   my sex drive did
 not die at birth   though i'll admit judging from the past
few years   it may be flagging
a sure sign though when i'm chatting up a strikingly sophisticated
woman whose eyes gazing into mine on every word
suddenly cross and her chin slips off the palm of her hand
with a jerk   she stretches   yawns and says
" will you please fuck me before i fucking fall asleep"
is a hint somewhat more difficult to overlook
anxiety sets in a bit   a major player in the world
economic crisis   european union   global markets
i myself tend toward a little anxiousness and
i   wonder

BLACK HOLES

don't believe what they say about black holes
they don't even believe it   they can't even get
the math right
in such circumstances   when scientists talk
their verbiage is called conjecture

black holes are unknowns surrounded by event horizons
they are not in agreement about what an event horizon
is   what it's good for   what really happens there
do your own math   i did and this is what i found

black holes are not holes   if they were holes
they would be flat on top   all diameters from all
points on the event horizon would connect
on either side as straight diameter lines
black holes are really spherical   get this   because it
enables them to satisfy their huge appetites   (hunger pangs)
from all directions   and what do they hunger for?
you guessed it (you're pretty good at this)
dark matter *and* dark energy   i theorize it takes a lot
to stay ahead of the scientific community
all the rest   stars and galaxies   flotsam and jetsam
and other stuff is all gravy or just a nuisance
if black holes suck up all the dark matter and energy
all other matter will become a round ball whose gravity
is so intense it will collapse under it's own gravity
into an infinitely small sphere
with infinite mass which will   *E=mc square*
and cause a very big bang   annoying a lot of people
this will take 5000 years according to inca scribes
assume this count has started over since may twenty-one
two thousand eleven
do the math   you will see

here is something you didn't know about black holes
if you jump or fall into one   you will fall
a long time and not reach bottom
but find yourself under a huge rock nearly at the bottom
but not quite   (even if you do the math you'll not find
the bottom for it doesn't exist yet in or out of math)
if you now look up   you will see gathered around the event
horizon   like the edge of a wishing well   all friends
relatives   the curious   the inquisitive   the bored
and others you don't recognize   some looking some staring at
the rock and only see a pair of comic eyeballs starring back
now if you should want to join them   you must
do the math   you will have to swallow the rock
to get out from under it   get it all
past your lips and teeth and gums and gulp it down
all the way down
now a deep knee bend and spring up with all your might
with the aid of a full arm stroke
swim for what you're worth   swim up all that distance
into all the shenanigans   all the combustions
all the affection forever in the universe
join them   have a coffee

TIME TO KILL

this morning
it is time to kill
willful   won-ton   throttling   slaughter
of those who skulked in the night   crept
in sunshine   rain and wind   crept unbeknownst
undercover   then rose above their betters
the preferred   the hapless few   who are no more
now it is roundup time   the day of righteous
indifference to the gasps and groans of their young
their old   their parents and seedlings
the beginning of a new birth of fragile greenery
                         a rebirth of new flora and fauna
where these will   ha-ha!   no longer be   but gonna!

TODAY, TOO

my mind is racing 20 miles an hour this morning
between a million   no   the more politically correct
billion things   achilles had only to choose between
this and that (not to belittle his conundrum   it was his
life and posterity in the balance   poor fellow)
but i have to choose between this and that and that and that
and this and that among other things!
for the first time in my life or the second i have made a
"to do" list
if i fail to complete it by noon i'll wait until susan is abed
and darken the living room of tv and stuff my ears with
the on/off switches of the cd player and tape deck
and there surrounded by my best friend   the dark
weep uncontrollably   really deep sobbing that clears my
digestive track of awful gas pains   sobbing as if i were
in a slumber room of a local funeral parlor watching
a replay of my failures through the gladioli mom's
favorite flower   all the possibilities gone awry for lack of
ambition   energy   understanding   clarity of purpose
one of the two
why don't i just sit down right now and quiver
chatter my teeth until exhaustion renders me helpless
because what i'm really excited about is a full 20 oz
glass of beer with dave and bill at the new italian
restaurant the name of which i cannot pronounce
but first i must get susan (she of the golden heart
and platinum spleen) a six-pack of bass ale
why should she   who with her goodwill chatter
and artistic generosity created a small hole or sphere
in which my life might expand and develop at its own
pace   was there ever such affection as this?
i think not!
if only i could envelope her in my skin where the
world seldom goes   and there at the bottom of our

tummies live warmly if a bit sticky yes and cramped
so while i'm "out with the boys" she is doing what she
does when drinking bass ale   burps   watches tv
maybe buries her face in amy's salt and pepper
until my return   begging forgiveness because the
girls were not invited this time   but maybe next. . .
don't finish that!   it could wipe "next time"
from the english language forever
well i've gotten this far with my "to do's"
if you fail to get this note stuffed in your milk bottle
i have (sob & sigh) failed in good intentions yet again
how about you?

ANOTHER MORNING

little amy   fifteen odd pounds of
salt and pepper hair and lightning-speed
quickness   and unconditional affection
stretched across my lap   on her right side
head on cylindrical pillow near my right hip
front paws in the air by my right thigh
body angles from right thigh across lap to
left hip   hind legs drape in the air near
left thigh   so light she floats in dreams
in the big chair in the big morning in the
quiet   everything   *quiet*
the breeze still asleep in the leaves   the sun rising
in the treetops   the rental neighbors
the steeple of the *new life tabernacle*
across the street   telephone poles   and finally
on the headstones in the *oakwood cemetery*
the other side of monroe street
they are full of anticipation   this could be
the morning   this could be the time
this could be the day   but no   the anticipation
waits for another day unabated   it's coming

the heart fills and empties fills and empties

the heart is a muscle or small group of muscles
gathered in the chest to pump life to the
far corner networks of the body   cleansed
by the liver   sucked into the lungs to gather
the silent thunder of oxygen for the return
the heart never thinks of this   it is work
the heart enjoys as it feels the quick thrill
            of travel

this is not   however   the heart's only employ
it is also the seat of emotions sent to guide the brain
with instructions how to arrange the innumerable
bits of information gathered for the purpose
analytical science with its intricate machines
denies this of course   they have some information
but be not quick to leave the expertise of the centuries
there are things in the heart it does not surrender
to flashing lights   maybe
it is this time of day clarity begins to ring
throughout the system   it says   "stay calm
everything is all right" after a night of tumultuous dreams
"everything belongs   everything has its place
all people are okay   though some are more
okay than others"   these reside in the seat of the heart
a little closer to the chest where they thrill to help us
keep our balance   coordinated rhythms of
beating and breathing and nothing more
now words begin to fail with   *love*   a word empty
of meaning and love until filled with action   the small daily actions
the huge actions of self-sacrifice which are not sacrifices
at all   after all
surely heaven must be like this
perpetual sunrise   filled with anticipations the
quick and the dead   the assurances and reassurances
it all works   everything fits   everything is okay   okay?

(POEM)

her lower lip is the back of a breaking wave
figuratively speaking   smooth   unhurried
from which emanate her consuming
grace and sensuousness
see how useless words really
are   in a furtive   sidelong   glance

WONDERS ARE THERE MANY

we frolic in the loose sand   the balls of our feet
doing the heavy work   laughing with sideway glances
only the tip phalanges loosely laced and sliding
against each other   it was the spring rising in us
i chose my favorite love song to serenade
from my favorite song and dance man
        wonders are there many
            none more wonderful than man
       his the might that crosses seas swept white
          by storm blasts
     his are speech and wind-swift thought
not much tune but she took my meaning
"i like the lilt" she says   our fingers lock tightly
we came on a small copse and caressed its shade
when we came upon a centipede   watch it
for hours   hand in hand   it does not move   we think it dead
we pick it up gingerly lest a bare fang nick us
and send us off on unearthly thrills
we admire its copper-colored exoskeleton
its tiny legs give us the reason
it had been taken by dance and not just any dance
but ballet   the princess of them all
it had purchased the toe-slippers with a thrill
never had it had such a number of things
and ribbons too   this is where it started to go wrong
it had slipped twenty pairs on but only tied seventeen
by that time it was august and it had starved to death
so many pink ribbons to wrap and tie
centipedes are not insects   but they live among insects
birds   voles   and clumsy chip monks who come along
with stuffed cheeks and trip over
the hiding place and leave the centipede exposed
to the vicissitudes of nature   natural selection and
reckless auto accidents   we wipe away a tear

centipedes have many pairs of legs that come two-by-two
though i have seen a centipede with an odd number
by nature or an evil little man-child who tortures things
it would advance and fall   advance and fall   saddest sight
i hovered over it to keep the birds away   till it fell into a bush
beside the path and safety   though the call of a brown thrasher
deep in the bush   and the catty call of a catbird gave me pause--
we cremated our dancing friend   found a like-new urn
that was lying around   dropped the ashes in
resumed our walk though not so gay to find a proper spot
to mix the ashes with the lake   how could we know the proper spot?
we wade out knee-deep and throw the urn's top further out
then set the urn upright gently on a wave   till nature take its course
how could that not be the proper spot   farewell we say goodbye
our wet feet collect sand as we walk more slow   till each then
both saw a vision in the clouds   we swear   the same for both
it was ringo star's sad eyes   smile and hooter face   dressed as for
a masquerade in a centipede suit from the shoulders down
his sad eyes turn to smiles to cheer us as he tosses his mop
from side to side and sings   *"you got that sand all over your feet but
uh-uh   baby don't!"*

A LOVE TRAVELOGUE FROM THE VATICAN TO THE SAVANNAHS OF AFRICA

it was an enormous surprise to see her here because we
had never met   happy coincidence!   she wore only water
from her cold shower   head bowed slightly she moves
toward me   throws my arms around her
and moves in just passed hug to amazing cuddle
little puppy sounds   "i want to be in your skin"
more puppy sounds
her goose bumps massage my smooth sighs and the bumps
become tiny suction cups sucking my skin
by this time the crowds had gathered
and my ears grew large as a bull elephant's
enfolding our modesty gently as the crowds turn to
the new pope on the balcony   arms out   palms up
in supplication   as he teleports us to
the elephant grass on the african plane
makes him eligible for beatification
i choke and cough like a three-pack-a-day
it is hot and dry even for the dry season and drought
my ears had been covered in dust and now we were covered
or i was covered for as my eyes cleared i could see she had
changed into a pink chalk-stripped suit with muddy chalk stripes
no   her shower water had combined with dust
to stripe down her skin and ankles to puddles she tried to cover
with her feet   humiliation moves her toward me again
past hug and cuddle   "i want to be in your skin still"
puppy snuggle sounds   tiny mouths again
yes we both weep a little   she for love and happiness
i for there is no clean spot to rest my lips

HE UNDRESSES A PART OF HIMSELF
HE THINKS

he undresses a part of himself he thinks
with tough   direct   self-realizations
staring at himself while shaving
"drunk on a weird mixture of selves
you are more stupider than ever
the more you learn and learn   the behinder
you get under the aegis of ignorance
oh you think you'll go more than half way
with affections as genuine as genuine this time
but you never knew how and still don't
though you walk on air with tightened chest
you jumble fear and honesty   reach out
step away   stay where you always are
you are so obvious in false confession
your comfort and solitary footing
hug all around at a distance
stupid   you are still so obvious as a can of milk
between two mirrors   *odd-infinitum* you
so obvious the ancient hellenes knew your story
long before you appeared   a gleam in the eye
drink receding from your dry throat
the golden fruit beyond reach
save for your fingertips   wet-brain
riffle 'em as you may   it ain't in the deck
it is not possible
you can *ever* be tee-totally honest"

AND, WELL, SO, WHAT ABOUT LOVE?

and   well   so   what about love?
by which we mean?
love
first of all is self-love   "i deserve to live
and have more than my share of what i love"
for example food   clothing   money   etc.
which leads to self-indulgence   lying and cheating
which ultimately leads to self-loathing
withdrawing love from daily bread and all
which may lead to resurrection of self through
love of god   fellow man   and admission of one's bestiality
love of sex or sexual love which do not really seem
the same thing though the many may hold it so
blinded as they are by sex   good or bad
not true or false   true love enters here
because of forbidden sex   and is the
justification the sex drive requires societally
true love is most always first love
and is forever   given forevers are of varying lengths
just as there are varying volumes of infinities
true love is forever love
there is no "false" love   false love is non-existent
it is wrong and inaccurate to think false love exists
though this examination may be becoming too weighty
it someday may get somewhere
though not before it becomes suicidally boring
ergo

horse sense is a different thing entirely
its entomology is the "common sense" of a horse
to come in out of the rain   though its work
impulse may delay the fruition of staying dry
with the promise to itself that it may return
to work after the rain

only recently have we risen above our arrogant
self-deception of human intelligence and allowed the
possibility that animal intelligence exists
though this view is not widely or universally held
(witness "dumb as a post")
for those of whom animal intelligence does exist
the horse is a prime example   as are the pig or swine
and some breads of dogs   the horse has the advantage
here due to jonathan swift's promotion of its intelligence
in his well-known *history of gulliver's travails* in which
gulliver was rescued from his animal prejudices by
a friendly band of noble steeds
and now the times have made a breast of it
and also suggests "common sense" is a perfect *non sequitur*

ANOTHER YOU POEM

give over comfort food!
it makes you feel shitty later
physically   mentally   emotionally
where's the comfort in that?
to get beyond the initial stages
i think i'll take a big bite out of you!
such goodness must have a positive
effect on one's nature and goodwill
just what the world needs
more placidity
what's in it for you?   *just this!*
you'll be like lance armstrong in his
halcyon days   able to eat anything
and everything   our goal is not
anorexia   better comfort food than that
but you'll need a gigantic calorie count
because of my voracious appetite for you
see how this works?   splendiferous!
the ultimate pleasure   joy!   or
is pleasure the ultimate joy?
who cares?   we have both a-plenty
to go around
mmmMMMMmmm
to get beyond the initial troublesome challenges
i think I'll start by nibbling your *toes!*

SAY

say this is a new language
which you can and will learn
if you can negotiate the details
images   twists and turns of whim
the crazy meandering of lines
the careless enjambments
the uneven stresses per line
so you begin with joyous enthusiasm
soon you notice *umlauts*
out of the corners of your eyes
dancing and bouncing over letters
you look   and they are gone
when you resume your focus
they return with other figures
like little pointy hats
over slippery vowels
you ignore them and go on
as they go on as well
is the language trying to teach you
to increase your visual field?
you can't be sure so you   go on
soon vocabulary increases
exponentially   you are dizzy with
new understandings you don't
feel you understand
your mind has been taken over
by deep knowledges in science
philosophy   religion   and the
hemispherisity of brain function
the new thoughts are heavy
with emotions   you wish
you had not begun
still you go on   tears redden your
goitered eyes and cheeks

your nose runs
but now you have finished
to what purpose?   sadness is a
strange happiness
you are finished but to whom can you talk?
you cannot go back   unless you learn to
read the language backwards
which you can *do!* and sideways
and in and out
the language can be read in any and all
directions and eleven dimensions
though some dimensions contradict others
the contradictions are resolved in yet others

                soon you learn to enjoy solitude
it is a pleasure not to think but let the language
investigate itself   it conquers babel   humbles nimrod
it clears your throat and sinuses   cleans your teeth
prevents chapping of the lips
your hair is rich and curly again

WORDS

words are a tub of electric eels
sometimes shocking always slippery
all words are just metaphors except like
similes and other figures
most people think words are like bricks
you can build a solid wall of conversation
or contracts with them
wordsmiths know better
take an old chestnut like "love"
it has so many connotations and denotations
it expands like a weather balloon to
dizzying heights   then explodes and fades
saying perhaps "someday you'll need me
and i won't be there-- here"
maybe the best way to think of words
is a flat rock skipped across a quiet pond
with each skip a few bits flake off
until it can no longer skip and just plops and
weaves its way slowly to the bottom
wait! wait! turn that up!
i love this song!

WINTER DREAMS

i open the cabin door
wolf tracks in the dust
of the single path that leads
to a place from which you can reach
 seney and as much civilization
as one needs   tavern   general store
gas pump
wolves don't wait around long
in the warm months
the heat of the day will be on them
too soon
in the cruel months i open the door
and find them curled tightly together
under the snow like stones
they rise slowly   stretch
then begin to weave in and out
smiling   peonies blossoming
from their mouths
each head careful not to lift too high
out of place and spoil the greeting
while continuing to weave
rubbing against each other
slack-jawed tooth kisses exchanged
renewing the pack identity
slowly the alpha male wades
 through the bob-and-weave bodies
his confident gaze captures my eyes
casually the lids open and close
the contact between us holds
don't dream up silly stories about us
they say   *we go where we belong*
our only rule
i step aside in acknowledgement
watch as they enter and arrange themselves
before the fireplace

SOGGY FOG MORNING

the patches of snow on the highest hill
in the oakwood cemetery   reminds me
of a slender little indian pony i once had
brown and white with blonde hooves
she was wild of course   there were lots
of wild ponies in those days
but she was special
most days she wouldn't let me ride
so we would graze side-by-side until dusk
other days she would chase me until i climbed
on her back   we would ride like the wind
lone ranger and silver style   all afternoon
there never was such a love again
on those days i would whisper in her brown ear
"you fill my heart with *fingerlings!*"

RICHARD POEM

i always wanted to write like this
smooth easy lines a quiet invitation
to a reader to walk awhile
the reader pleased and even eager
to hear a good story or a joke without a laugh
my lines don't sound like that   mine go
hey! get out of the way there i just went crazy!
especially compared to richard's
with him the reader gladly walks out beyond
city limits as if neither had noticed
through fields of grass never mowed
and mature woodlots that could make a sugarbush
the tough grass roots hold the sides of the path up
the sand a gentle curve for feet
friends forced to walk single file

LESSONS LEARNED AGAIN

known it all my life mostly
knew it this morning
walked by more than a week
two mole mounds several yards
a part connected by a molehill run
common sight in curtiss park
live and let live   leave them be i say
but this morning half-blind from
several inches of fluffy snow
and cutting a little more off
than usual to make fresh tracks
in the first real snow of the season
the moles and i come together
on a low side-hill right
at the toe
surprise? of course   always
heels over head   you bet
youthful balance gone
full-face lead and *still*
my nose makes a lousy snowplow

INVITE

every week richard and i would invite
bill stafford to join us for breakfast
we even offered to pop for the first one
but he never came
richard thought he was holding out for two
but that didn't sound like bill to me
we especially like his poem
traveling through the dark
it works perfectly on all levels
we felt obliged to tell him
how gratified we were
i even memorized it
but could never recite it all the way
through without bawling
richard and i put our telepathic heads
together over coffee at the milan big boy
hooked pinky fingers
and hummed eyes closed
we finally determined to our satisfaction
the magnetic lines of force
were in some unnatural way
dismantling our communiqué
somewhere over the mississippi

HERON IN THE HURON

well   it's not the huron but the saline river
that winds its way through curtiss park
and floods the park and the ball diamond
tucked in back by the wilderness area
every spring   you wouldn't want a house there
i just thought of the huron river because
it was across the road from huron high school
where i taught for many years
anyway the river is about four inches deeper
this morning after rain and snowmelt
still not too deep for the "big fella"
to continue fishing for breakfast
the big fella is the male heron of the pair
who spend most of their time year round
stalking the river with great dignity
no matter how muddy
he has a few small quills that jut
straight back from the top of his head
amy and i come up behind him where
the river turns right if you're walking south
(amy is a seven-year-old miniature schnauzer
fifteen pounds of pure energy under her silver
hair--schnauzers have hair   they don't shed)
quickly he regains his dignity   spreads his wings
as if to show them off   flaps and lifts straight up
out of the water at his leisure
looking back over his shoulder as if to say
"you earthbound creatures lack all sophistication
so crude   slovenly   and   boring"

COFFEE-STAIN BROWN

coffee-stain brown is my favorite color
on any background   though white is a bit garish
my eyes are blue but they should not be an issue
like every boy i swore when i got big
i'd eat all the chocolate i wanted no matter what
and i do too   my taste did change from
childhood milk chocolate to the more sophisticated
and expensive dark dark chocolate
my taste widened too to include imported nutless
nougat   especially at holiday time with peppermint
the potato is another childhood favorite
that has not waned   baked   boiled   home fries
french fries   ("american" fries?   *pituy*!)   hash browns
but what is with the curly fries with flavoring
salted on?   the delicious potato with artificial
flavoring? what can you be thinking of my
countrymen?   and the simple delightful chip
down home potato chip   aunt emma liked them
scooped with butter   but even as a child i
rejected that   what could be better than the
simple kettle cooked chip with the proper
measure of salt?   the potato needs nothing
more   i'll not dirty my tongue with the foul
flavorings commercialism has added
i'd have such people horse-whipped by the thumbs
and left with toes dragging in the harvest dust
another favorite since my childish days is the
potato scone   homemade   warm and dripping
with butter!

TUESDAY I THINK IT WAS

tuesday i think it was
but it didn't have to be
it could have been french
we met over drinks at the eiffel tower
i drank with a quick dignity
patrons thought i toasted fluttering eyes
our waitress secretly explained to all we were in love
surreptitiously we became the center of giggles
and thinly swallowed guffaws
truth is i was terrified
afflicted as i was with acrophobia
i drank quickly till acrophobia no longer came
trippingly on the tongue
then closed my eyes as half a dozen lovers
helped me to the safety of the elevator
while you   to avoid embarrassment
but to prove you could do it you said
took the stairs

THE DAY BEFORE MY SEVENTY-SEVENTH BIRTHDAY

wake up 2:00 a.m. on the button   mouth and throat desert-parched
all the way to the navel and maybe beyond   water water
surprisingly only two gulps do the trick   2:30 a.m. i give up and
get up   stagger just a little   go down stairs   find my body in the
kitchen trying a bay's english muffin   it brings us together
warm up a mug of coffee from yesterday's second pot   make a fresh
pot   head for the new big chair at the far end of the living room
determined for some unknown reason not to read this morning
lamp stays off   try to find a movie on tv determined not to watch
one of the *dragon tattoo trilogy*   seems i'm very combative this morning
i'm pretty sure i'm addicted to the swedish version   a good time for
cold turkey   finally come across a movie titled *sylvia* i've been
ignoring for several weeks   *who is sylvia?*   i think
time to see what it is all about   almost a jackpot
Sylvia is Sylvia Plath   as the lead says   "Poets Sylvia Plath (Gwyneth
Paltrow) and Ted Hughes (Daniel Craig) have a whirlwind courtship
but their union quickly dissolves due to Hughes's philandering and
Plath's insecurity."
the problem is gwyneth's face is so alluring i for one cannot relinquish
it to any part she plays   she is always gwyneth   and so i dose off
i awake as gwyneth is putting the children to bed and tucking them up
nice and snug   she then lowers the upper sash of the window about a
foot   steps back and smiles at the thought   then she goes into the kitchen
and seals the doors with tape   turns the gas up and sits in a straight back
chair and waits   here's the thing   the camera angle and the lens make
gwyneth look less like gwyneth than i've ever seen   in the next scene
a couple are in the children's bedroom picking them up and taking
them away still so sleepy they hardly know what
i don't know who these people are   they may be family friends
had i not dozed we would know   anyway the children are safe
later ted looks around and finds gwyneth's last manuscript
and still later by a year he supervises its publication
as an alternative a poet told me   "ted retired to the attic
and continued to write and publish gwyneth poems for years"

i think he was joking
about 4:00 susan comes into the living room and stands tentatively
in the shadows   "whacha doin'" i ask   "oh" she says
"i want to make a noodle dish for when karen comes back (from san diego)"
i say "okay"   susan goes back to bed
finally the gray morning sky rises to find me feeling like
a very calm storm
amy jumps in my lap

UPON THE POND

funny isn't it?
how when you're out walking
you loose your brain and unleash your
tongue and just let them run independently
how things come up?
"upon the pond" for example   appears a
gratuitous offering   repetitive sounds
yet no rhyme   three vowels   two of them
alike   two consonants repeated   but   but what?
we could go into grammatical constructions
but it is so irrelevant   two negatives make positive
but if you say "i ain't got no money" it would be
silly to ask for a fiver   wouldn't it?
some really go for that old latin stuff
i'm more patriotic than that

anyway the mallard pair easing away from shore
to the safety of middle pond are particularly
picturesque in the calm sprinkle of drops
upon the pond   and the rain does its part
to make this a totally dizzying dalliance
each drop a perfect bull's eye

APRIL IN ~~PARIS~~ SALINE

i want the dictionary on the coffee table five feet away
but little amy   hammocked in a lap rug between my knees
counts on these extra zzzz's after waking to an empty bed
staggering down stairs and into the living room
sits under her ears   eyes wondering until able to focus
just exactly where i am so she can jump up
after this additional doze she will be ready for anything

so what is a dictionary on the coffee table?   or the *mac os x*
for dummies in the basement that holds the answer just how to °
create a folder of perfectly arranged poems for the next book
to be emailed to two indispensable artists who await?   nothing

but as the deep french roast coffee from the press
begins to titillate the synapses behind my eyes   and words
begin to stir with snuggle sounds rubbing against each other
and once again discover the clitoris of my brain   they fill it
with hopes and promises of at *least* love if not sex

Acknowledgements

No matter the art form, dance, theatre, music, sculpture, painting, the artist's circle influences the product though the product has still the artist's undeniable stamp. Her circle is the frame of reference in which the world presents itself for interpretation, expansion and interpretation. It is my belief that poems and poetry work the same way. By the time one reaches one's seventh decade and nears the eighth the shape of the circle is very large though still a circle. Linear thinkers may imagine the shape more like a sausage, but let that go. I maintain this solipsistic universe is a spherical circle in which enormously important and talented people as well as mentally and emotionally challenged have been welcomed all along. It is a strange and loving place. This is not to say "this is how we do this." We still don't fully understand that, but we do appreciate everyone's contribution to the process. I do not deny disappointment in those who sobered up and cleared the mind and body of drugs who, in shock at the real dullness before them turned away because they had created something they enjoyed more than this new apparition before them. Yuck! I face the same shock every morning and have had to handle it. My affection for such ones is still deep in my heart as part of the process. So the following list of names and groups are most of those who did their best consciously or unconsciously to improve my works; the failures are not theirs. Too, there will be those not listed who may be more worthy than those who are. My apologies, the omission was not intentional. You are somewhat more quietly remembered here between the lines:

Richard Emerson McMullen, poet, mentor and grand exemplar; wife Susan who really did make all things possible out of the dark; immediate family, Carrigan and Woman, brothers Bob and Ed, they really did their best; son Jason and his lovely wife Karen; extended Carrigan family who first shaped the outside world; Jude Wilson (Press Lorentz) design; Maggie Dubris, the best writing student ever and now the world; Arlene Shy, husband John's Energizer Bunny, organization and endless friendship; Dave Stringer, friend, poet, colleague, for the poems with him now and in the future; Keith Taylor, poet, teacher, writer, but poet first, whose "eyes are the Mediterranean;" Warren Hecht, writer of fictions and now Catholic Deacon, and Andrew Rock (both of Street Fiction Press); Patrick Powers, friend and true original (Crowfoot Press); the Forsythe Junior High School faculty 1960-65 incredible teaching led by Leonard Hoag, Principle; Ann Arbor Huron High School English Department, 1970-75, chaired by outstanding teachers Jim George and later Gordy Johnston, proud to have been part of it. People of good will and friendship: John Nordlinger, Tina Hollowicki, Stan Bidlack, Bill Lavery, Carl Abel, Charlie Henry, Jordan Young, Tom Pendlebury, Bruce Cunningham, Tim Smith, Charlie Green, Jim Carras, Ed Klum, Jay Steilstra, Jim LaGoe, Bill Hunter, Jim Roland, Doug Mervis, Tom Raworth, Anselm Hollo, Ted Berrigan, Ken Mikolowski, Gordon Korstange, Bob Henry, Stanley and Norah Clegg, Jo and Marcus Westerby, Gary Gasser, Beverly Schlyer (Holland), Jack Depond, Jim Case, John Craig, John and Allen Schoolcraft, Jimmy Smith, Babs Losee, Tom Prince, Linda Hopkins, John Pheney, Sally and Desmond Ryan, Betsy.

About the Author

Andrew G. Carrigan was born in 1935 and grew up on a small farm near Battle Creek, Michigan. After serving in the navy and earning degrees at The University of Michigan, he devoted his professional career to teaching writing and to writing poems. He was an early champion of the small press movement in the Midwest, and has written unceasingly and published a number of collections celebrating the pleasures and puzzles of love and life. He lives with his wife Susan and their poetry loving pup Amy, in Saline Michigan.